SUSS!

The Easy Way to Sell Yourself, Your Product, Your Service and Your Ideas - with a little NLP!

by Russell Webster

RUSSELL WEBSTER

SUSS

A RETIRE EARLY PRODUCTION

Here is an outstanding fact.

Only 1% of the population of the modern world will ever be totally financially independent at retirement age!!

Another, rather more worrying, fact is that 95% of the same populations will require some State help at the same age.

Why is that?

The reasons are numerous: from illness to laziness. Yet if we had to pick just one reason it would be that the vast majority of people surround themselves with the wrong influences – the wrong environment.

In this instance the 'wrong environment' is the people you surround yourself with, the TV you watch, the books you read.
If, however, you mix with successful people you will gradually learn all of habits they have, from setting goals to taking the right kind of actions. You will also find that opportunities start to come your way.

In the absence of such people to bounce off then you simply MUST devour as many books, audio books, videos as you possibly can. We can help you with this!

We have made our books bite sized so that you can read them quickly and take the main points out of them. Our audio books are a great way to fill your mind with great information whilst you are travelling, and our Videoliminals are simply ground-breaking!

More about our exciting range of products at the end of this book.

SUSS

Also please visit our website -

www.retireearlyproductions.com

info@retireearlyproductions.com

It only takes one small piece of information to totally change your whole life!

The Retire Early Team

ABOUT THE AUTHOR

Russell Webster describes himself as an entrepreneurial version of Stephen Fry. He is an eclectic creator of new ideas and new concepts, widely published as an audio book writer and narrator, and an accomplished speaker.

In the late 1980s his first venture was to conceive, design and construct one of the UK's recording studios - The Slaughterhouse, which gained huge notoriety for recording the first Happy Monday gold album and visitors such as Brian May from Queen.

Music always was and still is one of his great passions, along with a voracious appetite for knowledge in all fields of psychology from Freud and Jung right up to Bandler and Grinder who pioneered NLP (Neuro Linguistic Programming).

After losing the studio in a fire Russell took time out to write his own music and become qualified in NLP.

He then pioneered a new type of audio book, of which he wrote several, narrated them himself AND added music underneath the spoken word. This was a great success and he has sold hundreds of thousands worldwide. They still sell just as well today.

Strangely enough it was when he finally wrote Seven Secrets (along with creating a musical score for it with a friend) he learned why he was only being moderately successful and made a huge change in his life by moving to London and launching a new business in the training field.

By applying his own principles to his new business he very quickly became wealthy. Then, when his marriage failed, he let the whole thing go so that he could be near his children.

After a topsy-turvy few years (to put it mildly) he spent two years writing his first actual book – SNAFU, which stands for Situation Normal All F***** Up. Although it was written as a novel it is quite a deep book. It delves into both success and failure and is best read by people who want to become counsellors or therapists. You do also find out a lot more about Russell, and the impact his childhood had on him. And on others.

Then, recently, he noticed that something really was, in his mind, heralding the total breakdown of the traditional family – console games and apps. His own children could hardly tear themselves away from their iPhones, iPods, iPads, and X-Box game long enough to say hello to him. He looked around him and found that this was widespread - so many children were no longer communicating with their parents in the way that children used to.

So, in 2015 he set about creating a board game. Yes, a traditional board game called THE FAMILY GAME - with Brian Brain's National Curriculum.

It is live and available now on Amazon and, fortuitously, it brought him together with a long-standing friend, Peter Aldred. Peter not only loved the game but also loved all of Russell's audio creations.

A partnership was formed in 2016. That partnership is called Retire Early Productions. As well as turning quite a few of Russell's audio books into 'real' books Peter and he came up with an exciting and ground breaking new concept called Videoliminals – combination of the spoken word, relaxing music and video.

You cannot keep a creative person quiet for long!

RUSSELL WEBSTER

ABOUT THIS BOOK

This book was first written as an audio book some fifteen years ago at the turn of the Millennium. It was extremely ground breaking at the time as, along with a friend Archie B, they wrote a complete musical score to fit alongside the voice of Russell.

It was so well received that it sold over 100,000 copies worldwide and continues to sell till this day on Amazon and various other outlets.

It is not crammed full of CLOSING TECHNIQUES like so many other sales books.

Yet it is crammed full of modern day techniques (a lot of NLP) that give you a much clearer understanding of how to create rapport with people and how to gain a real understanding of what truly makes people buy into you and your product or service.

RUSSELL WEBSTER

FOREWORD

I was always a good salesman because I got on well with my clients and gave them a great service.

However, I cannot ever begin to tell you how effective I really became after studying NLP. To me it is total cutting edge technology.

James Russell Webb

ACKNOWLEDGMENTS

To my brother Brad, who, over the years, has consistently helped me with proof-reading, editing and formatting.

SUSS

DEDICATION

I dedicate this book to the child that still resides in most of us. We all had such great dreams but most of us lacked the knowledge or drive to fulfil those dreams. Yet, it is never too late!

CHAPTER ONE

I just happened to be in the car showroom while my friend was paying for his car being serviced. On the windscreen of this silver car was its price tag, some £20,000. Below the price were the monthly repayments: approximately £250 per month for two years. I would say that my mental arithmetic was better than average and it just didn't compute. So I stood there, cogs whirring and scratching my chin for a moment trying to figure it out.

Well it must have been the chin scratching: for a long time known as a buying signal. The next thing I know there is a salesperson stood next to me saying "Are you interested then?"

Quite frankly I was not. Yet the way in which he asked me determined that even if I had been interested he was not going to sell it to me. So before he even launched into his sales pitch I was on the back foot or the defensive. He proceeded to then hamper his cause further.

"It is a lot of car for your money."

What happens if I don't like big cars, I thought. I also didn't feel too comfortable about suddenly having to think about parting with my hard-earned money. I stepped back a pace or two.

Unaware of my body language he continued "It does nought to sixty in nine and a half seconds!" No doubt intending to impress me further with his sales prowess and knowledge of what I liked in a car. Having never met me before and not bothered to find out much about me he was making a few assumptions based upon **his** belief of what makes a good car.

Nought to sixty in eight and a half seconds, I thought. I wondered how I might feel about a drop in performance in comparison to my present car, and quickly decided that this car would never be for me, whoever the salesman was.

"Guess what insurance group it is?" he asked, smugly.

I wasn't really in the mood for quiz shows, and I didn't give two hoots as to which insurance group it was.

"I haven't got a clue I said" not really warming to this fellow at all.

"Would it surprise you to know that it's only a group fifteen?"

"That's quite interesting" I replied, because I couldn't think of anything better to say.

I think he thought he had me hooked then. He asked me what my current car was, and, having informed him, he swiftly pronounced that I was definitely going to save a fortune. Also that the fuel consumption figures were going to impress me. (He knew me very well by this stage).

Then he started going for the kill. "Doesn't it look great in silver?"

I really didn't want to pee on his bonfire too much, but I really don't go for silver cars personally. I don't mind other people's silver cars; I just don't want to own one myself. So I changed the subject and asked him how the repayment figures work. He informed me that after the two years repayments there would be a lump sum payment left, whereby I could either pay it off to own it or I could use the residual value as a trade-in allowance.

Very neat I thought. Hire it for two years and then have a vehicle that is worth less than you owe on it.

One of my personal values was that I liked to own my cars as quickly as possible.

He said "What a great way to buy a car hey?"

He really knew how to **suss** out his potential buyers didn't he. I quickly used the polite form of don't call me I will call you, and asked him for his business card. Of course I thanked him for his help, and then my friend and I left.

On the way back to the car I told my friend Steve that I was actually considering a change of car, and that had the salesman asked a few sensible questions at the outset, created a little rapport with me, sussed me out properly and put me in a more receptive frame of mind then he might have made some mileage with me. Not with that particular car but as a potential customer for a different car more suitable to my requirements.

Before we nearly got run over by a London bus and distracted onto another subject I told him how many classic errors the salesperson had made, especially his opening line which closed my mind straight away.

Steve asked me what line might have made me more receptive. My answer was this: if the salesman had come up to me, with a nice smile on his face and said something like "Have you been thinking about the possibility of changing cars recently" then he would, without threatening me in any way, have opened my mind up into `possibilities' and `changing cars' mode and received his first YES from me.

Known as YES TAGS they are an important way of placing a potential customer in the right frame of mind. Had he continued from there and asked me what type of car I was currently driving, what I liked about it and what was important to me personally in a car then he would have been on a much better track.

However, this audio is not about cold selling, nor is it about YES TAGS, BUYING SIGNS, OVERCOMING OBJECTIONS, HURT AND RESCUE TECHNIQUES, PSYCHOLOGICAL RECIPROCITY, THE SILENT CLOSE AND OTHER SUCH CLOSING METHODS OR ANY OTHER SUCH TECHNIQUES, all of which have their definite uses.

It is however about the fundamental framework around which all successful selling must take place.

Whether you are already selling for a living and want to increase your commission cheques or you are about to embark upon a new career in selling or you simply wish to learn how to sell yourself to people or influence them a little more proficiently this framework will never change: you will simply become better and better at each little sub-component within the framework.

CHAPTER TWO

When I started my own sales career at the age of twenty one I really was as green as they come. At the end of the first day I was ready to quit, my baptism truly being of fire. The circumstances in which I had to sell were of the primeval sort, ten salesmen lined up like hunters trying to sell a car to some innocent, unsuspecting soldier on the way to do some shopping in his local NAAFI shop in Germany.

You can still witness a similar type of operation if you go away on holiday to a popular sunny resort, young sales people lined up by the road side attempting to sell you tickets to something or other; maybe go-carting or a visit to a time-share viewing.

Early that evening I sat pondering my lot over a glass of cool German beer. An intimidating and frightening day's work, no human contact with the enemy, the other salesmen that is, and not even a sniff of a sale. What else could I do for a living? How was I going to pay my rent? How was I going to eat?

It's amazing how life seems a little different when the fourth or fifth beer has hit your stomach and started affecting your brain chemistry. I wasn't a quitter. So I decided to stick at it and learn as much as I possibly could about selling. I talked to as many people as I could, as there was not much literature on the subject in the average German library. Everything pointed to closing the sale. That seemed to be the key. The techniques and process of actually breaking down the customer until you could write up the order.

To this day I still hear people talking about a certain close and other special closing techniques. Everyone seems besotted with the order taking element of the sale and seems to blindly ignore the process that must take place before they can even dream of taking an order.

Since those early days of my own sales career I have sat in on many sales presentations, with members of my own sales team, and time and time again witnessed this headlong rush to get to the close, quickly trying to overcome objections like papering over the cracks on the wall. Sometimes it works, often it does not. Have you ever been in the situation where, from the moment of entering your environment the salesperson appears to have nothing else on his or her mind other than closing you into their product? How do you feel when that happens?

I have seen great salespeople and poor ones. There was a time when I used to sit totally in awe of those people that could talk the proverbial hind legs off a donkey. You must have come across some of them; they could sell sand to the Arabs or ice to the Eskimos. What great salespeople they are. Or are they?

They may close more sales than most, write up more orders than most, but they don't always stick: another sales term to describe the element of staying sold until the product is delivered. There is a sales syndrome called Buyer's Remorse that afflicts many of their targets. After the party is over you realise that you have been railroaded or convinced to sign on the dotted line.

However, it was really not the product that you wanted, or you really could not afford it, or someone was going to be upset by your decision, or you forgot about your friend who sells a similar product. So you cancel the transaction. It doesn't affect the salesperson too much because he is used to it. He or she is the mud on the wall type; some of it always sticks. On to the next prospect.

CHAPTER THREE

The truth is, in my opinion, that there is no such thing as a great or a poor salesperson: there are simply great people persons.

The massive distinction, between a sales person and a people person, that I would like to make here, is that some eighty percent of all sales come from people that the potential consumer likes or is a friend of. People buy people! To become a great salesperson you therefore have to become a great people person. Doesn't that make more sense and also sound somewhat less daunting?

Nowadays my stock answer to those who say they are not closing enough deals is quite simply this: if you are not closing enough sales then you are not opening enough sales properly and then you are not asking enough of the right questions.

Nine times out of ten it draws a blank, quizzical stare. It throws a lot of people because it goes against the doctrine they have been used to: talking and closing. Whilst I was writing this script the phone went.

"Mr Webster?"

"Yes"

"My name is..........."

He then read his spiel from his script for two minutes solidly, without stopping whatsoever, until he eventually said "Do you think this might be of interest to you?"

I said "If I could show you a way of selling your product to me, and generally enhancing your success rate, would you be interested in finding out how?"

Totally thrown he hesitated and then said "Yes"
I asked him quite a few more questions and we had a really good chat. He then pre-ordered a copy of this audio. I didn't fill his advertising space, but mainly because it really was not suitable for us. I am sure that I will hear more from him.

In my opinion it isn't the talking and closing method that works at all. It is indeed the antithesis, the opposite that works: opening and asking questions. It is how you start and then where you go from there that makes a great salesperson.

CHAPTER THREE

If, right at this moment in time, every object around you suddenly started to change colour and shape then you might temporarily suspend your beliefs about the laws of physics. Try it for a moment and notice how it feels, how different things might look and how things could also possibly sound much different.

As you do this you might choose now or very shortly to notice how it feels to have an open mind. This open mind will help you to take this information in as if it were the first sales lesson you have ever had. That same mind of yours functions most effectively when it is as open as an umbrella. It will allow you to appreciate and remember that there are three phases to any sales meeting: somewhat akin to every event that has ever happened and ever will happen in your life. There is the before, the during and the after.

Let us start with one of the areas most often overlooked by the majority of salespeople: the before. If you understand the territory to be chartered before you set sail then you are far less likely to fall off the edge. If you were the commander of a group of forces due to attack someone`s territory the first thing you might do is send the scouts into the terrain to suss out the territory.

You would also use your intelligence services to provide you with as much extra information as possible. Indeed the motto of the British Army Intelligence Corps is Manui Dat Cognitio Vires, which means: Knowledge gives strength to the arm.

Think back to when you were at school, to a time when you were due to walk into the examination. Your chances of passing those exams were down to one thing more than anything else. How much homework you did and how well you did it.

Successful selling is no different. How much more confident might you feel going into a sales presentation knowing exactly what sort of person or people you were going to be meeting. If it is a company how would you feel about some inside information on the company`s short, mid-term and long term strategic and financial planning on your product or range of products.

Cast your mind back 15 years or more and pretend for a moment that you represent a company that sells fax machines. Just try and live this scenario for a moment. You are that person right now. You are about to enter the office of the person responsible for purchases.

As you are entering another person is leaving. You notice the Microsoft sticker on the side of his oversized case but think little of it. You make your sales presentation, yet leave without the order. In fact you did not really think you were anywhere near the mark and are slightly bewildered. Have to polish up on your closing techniques hey!

On the way out you notice the receptionist has a small box on her table that she is starting to unpack. Written on the side of the box in large writing is the word MODEM. The penny starts to drop and of course you are right. This company has a new policy of replacing all faxes with fax-modem add-ons to their PC's. Oh for a little advance information.

Move forward to today. This time you are selling state of the art hard drive storage solutions. They are great value for money and superbly well built. You make your presentation and indeed you are the only rep they are seeing. You get on well together and feel pretty smug about getting this huge order.

YOU DON'T!

The Company was well switched onto disaster management planning so they made the decision to store everything in the cloud!

Whoops!

Next time just SUSS out the territory a bit better and anticipate where the world is heading with yours or equivalent offerings.

CHAPTER FOUR

There are two areas that you need to suss out before you enter the terrain. Firstly you need as much information about the company and the industry that they are in as possible. What its plans and fiscal policy is with regard to your product and also what its competitors are doing.

The second area is the individual him or herself, starting with the most fundamental question of all. Does this person have the authority to buy or purchase your product or service?

Let's first deal with the Company itself and start with a trip down to the local library. Most Companies, by law have to file their end of year information with Companies House and this information is available on microfiche. There is some very useful information available here, ranging from the Directors and their shareholding within the Company to the size of its turnover over the last three years.
Some libraries also hold information on which Companies have had Court judgements against them, and if not, then there are agencies that do have this information. This information could be useful in more ways than one.

Many Companies have a corporate brochure that will tell you nearly everything you need to know about them. When they started, where they have been, where they are going, who is responsible for what and so forth?

When ringing up to make your appointment is also a good opportunity to glean a little more information. Receptionists and secretaries are always a mine of information and normally glad to impart some of it, without being disloyal and giving away confidential information. Indeed making an ally out of the secretary can be a very wise move. If you do it well you will have someone routing for your cause from the outset. A lot of bosses have good relationships with their secretaries, and are likely to be influenced by a secretary saying that you seem like a nice person.

All you have to do is ask questions. Questions related to your task in hand. How many employees do they have? What is their company policy on XYZ? Find out as much information as you can, for it will assist you enormously.

Ask about the person whom you are going to see. Does he or she like quick appointments or long ones? Have they been in that job for a long time or are they rising meteorically up the corporate ladder? Does he or she make the decisions or do they need to ask someone else. This is very important because you may not even have the appointment with the right person.

When the moment arrives to turn up for the appointment you will have a basic understanding of the company, and its turnover, the size of their potential market, who its competitors are and what they are investing in. If you have a good understanding of their product, their method of sales and marketing and their marketplace as well as some information on their internal systems you will be in a very advantageous position. If you also have some basic information about the individual with whom you are going to have your meeting, do you feel you might be just that little bit more confident, that you have just a slight edge.

All you have to do is a little homework and suss it all out beforehand. This will give you both a tremendous knowledge advantage and also should serve to increase your own confidence. It's a great way to start your meeting.

CHAPTER FOUR

You don't get a second chance to make a first impression. That's the adage. It's not always true, but it is hard to reverse an initial bad impression. The modern human inheritance of our pre-historic ancestors is the need to exact a quick and accurate judgement on whether others are friend or foe. It is genetically inherited, is known as the fight or flight response and is designed to protect your well-being.

Perhaps not as necessary as it was thousands of years ago it does still however govern the opening of the majority of first meetings, whether that is attempting to fit into a group of potential new friends, a potential new partner in a relationship or in your business dealings. People have an in-built need to make a quick assessment of you!

Dressing the part, looking the part, and acting the part are as important as being the part and, as we will come onto, listening the part, to make that first impression.

To do this you have to be in the correct state of mind. To help you remember the four step process of the meeting itself we are going to use the acronym SUSS as a reminder. The first S of SUSS standing for your state, your **state** of BODY and your **state** of MIND:-YOUR ATTITUDE.

There is a saying that goes everyone loves a winner, and is true of the majority of people. The first indication of whether you are a winner or not is your external appearance: how you dress and how you carry yourself: the aura that you give off.

SUSS

How you dress and the other elements of your physical state or appearance should be a matter of common sense. Pay attention to it for you will never climb the ladder of success dressed in the clothes of failure. Check that your clothes fit and don't worry about wearing your best suit; it is an investment in being able to buy lots more of them. Check your hair cut and other elements of your appearance such as your fingernails; it makes the difference.

Try and avoid loud flashy items of clothing, and take off over-the-top jewellery. Many people regard loudness as unsavoury or even threatening. An important distinction that I would like to make here is that it gives your potential client the chance to make a decision you most certainly do not want them to make; the decision of thinking to themselves that you are not at all like them.

Your internal state of appearance: how you come across as a person, your attitude or state of mind is the next dead giveaway. A false one won't do. It is like a veneer that will wear thin very quickly. The state of mind that I believe will serve both you and your potential client extremely well is one of being about to meet someone who may well become a lifelong friend: someone who you would wish to do things for and who you would hope would also do things for you.

Not only do I truly believe that this state of mind will assist you enormously but may well have the added bonus that you do indeed become friends. What a great way to do business in the future. Go to lunch with a friend, enjoy the food and the company and tidy up a little paperwork at the end of the meal, say a hundred new cars for the fleet.

What character attributes or mental state makes a great first impression and how do portray those attributes even when you have had a miserable day.

To an extent this is rather subjective and you may well choose you own. The state of mind I like to adopt is that I am about to meet the brother or sister of someone I used to have a very good friendship with. I am really looking forward to the meeting. I am confident, without being cocky and I am warm natured. I am eager to ask questions and I am a great listener.

I can learn a lot by listening and observing. People like me, and I fully expect this person to like me. Not only am I a nice person but I also deliver value and I deliver solutions as opposed to a product or service. I have a genuinely great smile. It is going to be an intriguing experience.

How do you create this state of mind or attitude, when are at the end of a not so good day or you would really rather be at home in bed with the flu. Or maybe you are quite simply terrified.
Let's start with confidence and let's do this right now.

CHAPTER FIVE

Imagine you are sat in a room full of people talking a totally different language to you; a room full of foreigners. How confident do you feel about picking up and understanding their language quickly? If you feel confident, then that's great. If you don't then you should, because that is exactly what you did as an infant. You interpreted a massive jumble of sounds and made sense of them. You learned to speak your own language didn't you? Think of a colour.

As you think of that colour think about something you do very well indeed, and it doesn't matter what it is. It could be riding a bike or knitting or mowing the lawn. It doesn't have to be elaborate....something simple will do. As you think about that thing that you do very well and also think of that colour then think of a time when you felt very confident about a situation. Maybe a subject that you are very knowledgeable about.

Think of a shape...any shape.

As you think of your yellow triangle or your red circle or whatever it may be for you then imagine too a time when you felt totally unstoppable and totally confident about a situation. If you can't think of one then just pretend that you could. Assume the body posture of someone who is supremely confident. How do they stand or sit.

Maybe you could pretend that you are your favourite confident movie star. As you now imagine your colour and shape in front of you on the floor and build up the intensity of your confidence inside you like turning an amplifier up full blast or a light inside you being turned on fully and a feeling that is becoming intensely pleasurable then step into your shape and allow it to engulf you and enjoy the experience.

Now step back again and notice how it feels.

Repeat the process with the other attributes that may be useful to you. Remember a time when you were very warm-natured and did something very nice for someone else. Build up the feelings, sights and sounds that were associated with it, praise yourself for being a warm-hearted person and step into your shape.

Remember a time when you were totally intrigued by someone and were totally enraptured by what they had to say. Build up the intensity of the experience and step into your shape.

Do this with all of the attributes that you think will help you. Practise it in a quiet moment as much as you can and next time you are about to enter a meeting just step into your imaginary shape or roll it out on front of you like a carpet . Allow it to engulf you.

Finally, remember that your mental state of mind will always reflect your physical state. The two are totally intertwined. Make sure that you are not standing in your shape and adopt the posture of a depressed person right now. Slump your head and shoulders and allow your facial muscles to adopt a sad, depressed look.

Without changing that posture try to imagine being confident and inspiring someone.

Now, shake it off. Stand tall. Smile, look up at the ceiling, feeling confident, feeling massively confident... and step into your shape.

SUSS

If you make a commitment to yourself to learn and practise this particular technique then you will learn how to change your state of mind at a moment's notice. Particularly when you most need to.

Remember to do it with your smile too. It is that most important representation of both your internal and external state. I believe that this poem says it all:

A smile costs nothing yet gives you much.

It enriches those who receive,

Without making poorer those who give.

It takes but a moment, but its memory lasts forever.

None is so rich or so mighty that he or she can get along without it.

A smile creates happiness in the home,

Fosters goodwill in business

And is the countersign of friendship.

It brings rest to the weary,

Cheer to the discouraged,

Sunshine to the sad

And is nature's best antidote for trouble.

Yet it cannot be bought, begged, borrowed or stolen,

For it is something of no value until it is given away.

Where some people are too tired to give you a smile

Then give them one of yours, as no one needs a smile as much
As he or she who has none to give!

Before we move on there is one final point that I would like to make about handshakes, which are likely the only physical contact that you will have, and can make a big difference with first impressions. Do not have a standard handshake. Of the three main types of handshake: the limp fish, the neutral and the vice, what is important is to return, match and compliment theirs. If you squash their limp fish with your vice they will immediately feel overpowered and very different to you.

If you place your limp fish into their vice the same applies in reverse, and they will once again feel as though you are very different to them. Start with the neutral handshake and soften or harden as necessary. It is the first chance you will get for the sub-conscious mind of the other person to make a quick assumption that you are similar to each other. The importance of this will become apparent as we continue into the programme.

CHAPTER SIX

The next letter in the acronym is U and it stands for Understudy. It is the key word to helping you do the next most important thing within the sales process, and also to making new friends. It is one of the keys to becoming a great people person; creating rapport with a total stranger.

It hinges upon one simple and indisputable fact: that people who are like each other tend to like each other. You can bend it and twist it any which way you like and it still has the same impact. Try it backwards. People who like each other tend to be like each other.

Have you ever noticed how two people who are in total rapport with each other seem to be almost copying or understudying each other? They are maybe sat at a table in a restaurant, facing each other, in an identical position, and probably quite close to each other. They are almost certainly talking at the same pace and even breathing at the same rate.

If you could just pretend for a moment that you were a passive observer in that same restaurant. You can see, hear and get a gut feel for whether people are in rapport with each other. A few tables off to one side is another couple. One of them has his or her elbows on the table and is leaning forwards.

The other person is sitting back in their chair, legs crossed, arms folded with one hand covering their jaw. That person is giving slow deliberate answers whilst the other person is jabbering away excitedly, words pouring out ten to the dozen, arms waving about quite rapidly. Do you think that they are in rapport with each other? No way Jose.

One of the great keys therefore, to creating rapport with a person, stranger or otherwise, is to understudy them, like an actor or actress must understudy someone ready to step into their role at a moment's notice, and be like the other person.

The starting point here is to understand that every one of you has a different method of communicating to yourself and to others. A different Mind Method.

The second point is to understand that communication itself is not just about the words that people use. Indeed, in external communication words are the least important of all. If you were a member of the opposite sex and I came up to you, wrapped my arms around you, gently stroked your back, looked deeply and lovingly into your eyes and said " I really hate you"......what message might you be getting. How important are my actual words?

The fact is that only seven percent of your communication is through the words that you use. A much larger percentage, thirty eight to be precise, is through the intonation and voice inflection that you use, and by far the most important part of your communication is through your body language: from your facial expression to your body posture, from your breathing patterns to your arm and hand movements.

If you were late home one night and as you first spot your partner who has been waiting for you they are stood there, quite upright, arms folded, scowling, eyes glowering and you can almost see the steam coming out of their ears then let me ask you a question. Do you need any verbal communication to get the gist of what is going through their mind?

What about that little eye roll that says "what a fool he is making of himself".   One hundred percent communication with one gesture!

As you now understand the importance of body posture and body language as well as the words you use and how you use them, let's go back to those Mind Methods.

Most of us interpret and process all communication through our three major senses of sight, sound, and feel. Nearly every one of you has chosen to adopt one of these three senses as you predominant method or vehicle to communicate and interpret your world. You are almost certainly a Visual person, an Auditory person or a Kinaesthetic person.

To recognise which of these three Mind Methods you have chosen to adopt then decide from the following questions which you might be:

Do you get an insight into things? Do you tend to have a viewpoint on certain matters? Do you like to get the picture?
Do you tend to talk quite quickly and use a lot of gesticulation? Do you say "I see what you mean??"
If this seems to be you then you are predominantly a Visual person.

Alternatively do you like to talk things through, get tuned into things? Do you say "I hear what you are saying?" Do things ring a bell?   Are you all ears sometimes?   Do you tend to listen to people's words to hear exactly what they are saying?   Do you speak at a fairly moderate pace and not use a lot of fast body language.

If this seems to be you then you are predominantly an Auditory person.

If neither of these two seems to fit you then you are most probably a Kinaesthetic person who likes to get a feel for things. Get hold of the situation and get a grasp on it. You probably like to weigh things up before you get a handle on it. As you are doing this you probably speak quite slowly and deliberately.

Many of you are a hybrid of all three of these, but are nearly always predominant in one or the other on given occasions. The critically important thing to realise whether you are trying to sell something or trying to make a new friend or even chat up a potential partner, is this: a Visual person, who likes to get from A to B quickly does not like the speed at which the Kinaesthetic person communicates and does **not** get a feel for you or your product. He or she doesn't know what you are going on about and wishes that you would get to the point.

The Auditory person doesn't like the Kinaesthetic person going on about feeling things and the Visual person seeing things. He thinks that they are both on a different planet and wants to tune into a few bits of language that he can interpret.

Whilst the poor Kinaesthetic, who is desperately trying to get to grips with the Visual person who is talking quicker than the speed of light, waving his arms around, spouting benefits and using a foreign language all the time, incessantly asking if he gets the picture,......... doesn't. He or she wants you to go away and leave them alone.

TO BE LIKED BY SOMEONE YOU HAVE TO BE LIKE THEM.

To create rapport with a potential customer you have to study them and then understudy them. In NLP, the study of communication, we call this matching and mirroring. When you enter another person's environment you need to fit into that environment as quickly as possible, otherwise you will stand out like an old grandfather clock in a modern state-of-the-art office suite. The quickest way to do this is to gain the trust and rapport of your potential client. To do this then communicate like them. Pick up their pace as if you were both going on a long journey together. They lead and you follow alongside.

The first thing to do is to adopt their body posture, every last bit of it. As they move and change theirs then so too should you change yours to match it. Match their facial expressions and any body movement. If they lean forward then you lean forward and if they start tapping the desk then pick up their rhythmic speed and tap your other hand or your knee at the same tempo and rhythm.

I know that this can seem like mimicking and possibly even manipulative, but just watch any couple who are in rapport with one another, like the two in the restaurant. As one of them shifts position so too the other will follow. This is rapport at the sub-conscious level and is the most natural of all.

If you repeat the same process for the speed and pitch at which you talk, the intonation you use and the words that you use your potential client's subconscious is saying to itself. This person is just like me. Remember that like people tend to like each other. Learn how to spot whether they are Visual, Auditory or Kinaesthetic and match their Mind Method. Use the same types of words and expressions and they will relate to you very quickly.

When you eventually master the art of picking up and matching someone's pace and Mind Method and being just like them you can then even lead them to pick up your pace. When you have total rapport you can then lead them elsewhere. You have gained their trust. Try this with someone you know. Pace them, match them and then lead them. Change a part of your communication and watch them follow you. If they do then you know you have rapport. This can also be a lot of fun.

CHAPTER SEVEN

The third letter in the acronym is S and stands for SEEK and I believe that the ability to understand and practise this is that which will set apart an average salesman from a great salesperson. It is the ability to seek information and then deliver solutions.

In the oldest book of wisdom of our time, the Bible, it is written "Seek and ye shall find". Much sales literature has been written over the years that is loosely built around the CONVINCE ethic; overcome this objection, that objection and convince them that yours is the right product.

If you can throw away all of your preconceived ideas about selling being a job of convincing and adopt the frame of mind or attitude that you are a seeker and not a convincer then I truly believe that you will write more orders than ever before and also that selling will become a much more gratifying and rewarding process for you and for your client.

So what are you searching for? You are searching for the dominant reason or motive that makes someone desire your product or service.

Nobody, but nobody, buys a car because they want a car. Nobody buys a conservatory because they want a conservatory. Nobody buys an investment or life policy because they want such a policy. Nobody buys advertising space because they covet advertising space. What they do buy is what it does for them. What value it creates for them in their life or for their business. What solution it offers.

I am going to say it again. Nobody buys a product or a service. Whatever your product may be, and that could simply be you yourself. People buy the value that a product or service offers. Not the means value but the end-value. The car itself is the means value. What it does for you is the end-value. This is the one that counts.

Think back to the last time you purchased a car. Something, some particular end-value made you purchase that particular vehicle. It may have been the speed it does or alternatively its fuel consumption figures. It may have been that you felt particularly safe in this car or maybe the interior made you feel a certain something.

It may have been that you could imagine certain people being jealous of your car, and that was important to you. It may simply have been that it was the right price and that was important to you. Whatever it was, something was important to you. There was a deeper reason, some end-value that motivated you to purchase that particular car.

It is hard to get all excited about spending one tenth of your income to own a piece of paper that says POLICY DOCUMENT on it. It is however possible to get excited about retiring early, going on a round-the-world cruise, and knowing that there will always be enough money and financial security to keep you in or enhance the lifestyle that you are used to.

For another person that same document may mean something totally different. It may create a totally different end-value. What does your investment policy mean to you? What end-value will it give you?

With the rather quirky attitude that many companies and individuals have toward off-the-page advertising, selling `space' in magazines or newspapers is not an easy business to be in. Or is it? Maybe it's a simple case of terminology.

Buying space does seem daft: there is loads of space out there, just look up toward the sky on a night-time. Buying increased Company profile or buying in business seems to make sense. Buying in customers and therefore income has to be winning concept. Buying in security for yourself sounds as if it may be worthwhile doesn't it?

Information therefore has to be of critical importance. In order to gain information you have seek it; you have to ask questions. Where so many sales people talk, the very best I have come across ask questions and then SHUT UP and listen to the answers. By asking the right questions and listening carefully to the answers you will gain all of the information you need to enable you progress to the final stage and take the order.

Just supposing for a moment that you sell conservatories for a living. You are in the home of the prospective client and you have gained a good rapport with them. You also know that they are a very visual person. What questions might you ask?

You don't have to be a genius to remember all of these, because there are basically only two. The first of these is "What is important to you". So the question goes "What is important to you about having your own conservatory?"

Let us say that the first answer is "I see it as somewhere nice to go on an evening".
Okay. So now you know that evenings in the conservatory are important to them. Do not think that this is their end-value: it's

only a half-way house. The next question to ask is this. "What does that mean to you?"

"Well, it means that I can get away from work, go in there and watch the world go by and gaze up at the stars at night"

Now we are getting there.   Notice too how all of a sudden he has gone all kinaesthetic. Let's ask the question again and add two important words from the hypnotherapist's dictionary: AS YOU. "As you see yourself sat there watching the stars at night what does that make you feel"

"Well, I just see myself totally at one with the world. It's when I do my most creative thinking too"

Bingo. This man doesn't want a conservatory. He wants to sit behind some glass, watch the stars, get in touch with himself and do some creative thinking.

You may have to ask more questions to build up the picture or the gut feel for this client. To do this simply ask the same questions. "What else is important to you about having a conservatory?"

"What does that mean to you?"

People love to talk, and be listened to.   It's one of the fundamental laws of psychology. Don't be afraid to ask lots of questions. Furthermore, they are now doing your job for you. They are telling you their deep seated reasons for wanting you product. They are literally selling it to themselves.

"Of all the things you just mentioned what is most important of all?"

SUSS

This question should tell what their highest end value of all is pertinent to your product. It is the most important piece of information you need. You are now ready to move on to the final stage.

CHAPTER EIGHT

The last letter in the acronym is another S.

But where is the C you might ask, if you are already a sales person. It all makes perfect sense so far, but what about the CLOSE. You have to close the deal don't you?

In my opinion the word should be eliminated from all sales training for ever. It is a really negative word. Who the heck likes to be CLOSED, locked in, strapped up...? How do you feel about having just been closed into a deal? It's no wonder many people get Buyer's Remorse a short while after being closed.

Of course you have to take the order: that's your job. Taking the order, however, is a much more pleasant set of circumstances then `going for the close' or `being closed'.   The traditional method of `closing' suggests a conflict: pitting your wits against theirs. It is far less threatening to think in terms taking an order to open up new possibilities. Surely that is what you are doing if you believe in your product or service; you are opening up a whole new world of possibilities for your customer.

I believe that this attitude or thought process will revolutionise your thinking and really increase your order taking rate.

To take the order there is one last thing you must do. You have to SATISFY someone's criteria for purchasing your product or service, and you also have to satisfy the ecology or the consequences of their decision.

If your potential customer is obviously chomping at the bit to order your product, because he or she likes you so much and has answered so many of the right questions that they have sold it to themselves then simply ask for the order. At this stage you may well have satisfied their criteria already.

Ask a very simple question. "Would you like to get the paperwork out of the way now, or in a moment or two?"

This is called a TIME BIND: a technique I have learned and adapted from the greatest neural linguist of our time, Milton H Erickson. It is so clever because it offers a choice. However the choice has the same end result. The choice is whether to order it NOW or in a moment or two. If they do not say yes there and then they have just agreed to say yes in a moment or two. You just have a few more criteria to satisfy before they make their decision.

However, many people are afraid of making decisions. Indeed most human beings dislike making decisions. Studies have shown that we suffer temporary insanity prior to making decisions. The reason for this is that most people have not considered the consequences or the ecology of the decision. Whether or not they can afford it. Whether some other person might be unhappy about the decision.

There are of course a whole host of consequences that may be on the mind of your customer. The consequence of the reliability of your product or the effectiveness of your service. Its shape, size, suitability, weight, packaging, colour, quality, reliability and longevity. It's quite a long list.

If you feel totally happy with the consequences of a decision that you have to make then surely you would make that decision right now.

Therefore, if your customer does not want to order straight away you have not satisfied his or her qualms about the consequences of the decision.

The next question to ask always starts with the same five words: WHAT WOULD HAVE TO HAPPEN.

Link these five words to their highest end-value, that we talked about earlier, and use words suitable to their Mind Method and phrase a question something like this:

"What would have to happen for you take the first step toward being sat in your conservatory, watching the world go by, being at one with things and being very creative?"

They will then tell you exactly what must happen for them to be able to make their decision. Listen ever so carefully to their answer for it will be full of clues. As well as having a Mind Method everyone has a set of Motivation Methods or mind methodologies as well.

They range from whether people need to do something for themselves or for the appraisal of others ... to whether they need their product to be like that of others or to be different.

The one I will briefly explain is the most powerful one of them all, and understanding and using this will give you a great edge.

Everything you ever do and every decision that you ever make is based around that which either gives you pleasure or avoids you pain. There are virtually no exceptions to this rule. In terms of Mind Methodology most people choose to make decisions based upon moving towards something pleasurable or moving away from something painful.

When you ask a question of someone they will, by and large, answer it in one of two ways. They will tell you what they do want or what they don't want.

"I want to do XYZ because it will give me ABC". This person moves toward pleasure.

Another person will say: "I don't want to do XYZ because otherwise I won't get ABC". This person moves away from pain.

One person will get in the car and drive half a mile because they enjoy driving. Another person will think of it in terms of 'they hate walking'.

These two methods of thinking are diametrically opposed to one another. It is important to listen to the wording of their answer and phrase your next question using their Mind methodology.

Answer one might be: "I would have to be sure that I wasn't going to be left in financial trouble". This is a moving away strategy. Your next question would therefore be "If I could show you a way to buy this product in a way that would not leave you in any financial trouble, would you then be ready to order it?"

The other answer might be: "I want to make sure that I can afford it". This is a moving toward strategy. You would phrase your question like this: "If I can show you how you can afford it would you then be ready to order it?"

Within both of these questions IF and THEN are also key words. They do need to be matched to either the moving toward or moving away strategy of your client to be most effective when handling so-called objections. Use these two words to overcome and circumnavigate any uncertainty your potential customer may have with regard to the consequence of their decision.

If you elegantly and sincerely lead your customer to a situation whereby they are totally happy and comfortable with all of the consequences of having purchased your product or service you will then be able to take the order. The important distinction here is that you have not had to leap over a series of fences and ditches on an obstacle course in order to close a sale. All that you have done is opened up a clear route together.

If you have done this particularly well then you will also have planted metaphorical daffodils along the route. These will then blossom into flower every year. They are your repeat business. Furthermore, your client will occasionally pick a bunch and give them to a friend. These are known as referrals and are the lifeblood of a long and successful career is sales.

CHAPTER NINE

Passivity of income has always been a personal goal of mine, and one that I would urge you to consider the merits of. It is one whereby your income keeps coming even when you are not working or able to work.

What happens when you are ill and Mohammed can't go to the mountain. Well the bottom line is this: if you have built a strong rapport with and truly delivered value to your client then you will reap the reward of their repeat business and receive a bountiful supply of referrals. You may have to ask for a lot of those referrals but they will come.

If you have created value and given true service before, during and after the sale you will never need another list of potential new contacts. How many times have you gone to a restaurant or to the movies or to seek professional advice on the advice or recommendation of someone else?

If you accept that much business is conducted in the same manner and also accept the premise that everyone knows at least two people to whom they would happily refer you, and that, based upon that good quality referral, even if they currently had no need for your services they would happily offer you another referral then you need never cold canvass again.

If you started today with that one satisfied client and turned that into two referrals and then the next day turned those two into four. How many potential referrals might you have by the end of a thirty one day month if you could simply double the amount from the day before? I know that you probably don't know the answer but if you did know then what would it be? Take a quick guess.

Rounding it down to a nice even figure the answer is 500 million referrals. Point zero one percent of that is still five hundred thousand.

From one totally satisfied client you can build an income stream for life if you continue to apply the same principals of doing your groundwork beforehand, using the acronym SUSS to remind yourself to create the right physical and mental STATE, UNDERSTUDYING them to create rapport, becoming a SEEKER and not a convincer; seeking information as to what they value in your product or service, and SATISFYING the consequences of them purchasing your product.

There is but one thing left to do. This one function or act can beneficially affect your repeat business and your quality and quantity of referrals. It is that so often ignored expression 'After sales service. Take the time to go around and visit your client after they have received your product or the service that you have provided is in operation.

Make sure that it is working properly. Offer them a little help if needed. Show them that you care and it will make such an extra difference. It is also a superb opportunity to ask for that first referral.

And finally, remember that this is a framework within which to work and that all of the points in this audio are guiding principles. Learning the finer points that fit into this framework will truly set you apart from the pack. Learning to adapt and be flexible in your verbal and non-verbal responses will give you that extra special edge. Not just in selling, but also in every human interaction that you will encounter, whether that is passing an interview, making new friends or finding your ideal life partner.

SUSS

Commit to understanding SUSS. Practise it with friends or strangers. Practise understudying; matching and mirroring them, and seek information as to what is really important to them. It is a great method of making conversation and making new friends.

In human cybernetics, the study of human systems interacting with themselves and one another it is he or she who is most flexible that has most control in any given circumstances.

If you think that you are not directly involved in the selling of a product or a service then please think again. Whether you are just leaving school or you are the chairman of a large corporation, or a single person looking for a partner or simply seeking to make new friends you constantly have to sell yourself aren't you? Flexibility is an important character trait to possess to enable you to use the principles of SUSS. Are you flexible?

I hope that you have both enjoyed and benefitted from this introduction to SUSS and that it will make a significant difference to both your sales performance and to all of your dealings with your fellow man and woman. If there were one over-riding message for me to leave you with then it is this: it is the value that you create for others in life that counts. The return will come as a pleasant by-product of that process.

Enjoy the process.

Introduction

A SHORT INTRODUCTION TO NLP

Neuro Linguistic Programming (NLP) is a mental programming model used to enhance the thinking of the human mind.

It was devised by Richard Bandler and Michael Grinder (NLP was originally developed as a means to investigate and replicate extreme human excellence).

It also drew heavily upon the teachings of Fritz Perl and Milton Erickson.

One of its great bedrocks is that THE MAP IS NOT THE TERRITORY.

The map is the world you live in and know, whereas the territory is the unexplored places in your mind.

- ✓ Increase the performance of an individual
- ✓ To reach a goal
- ✓ Overcome psychological disorders (i.e. anxiety, phobias, depression, etc.)
- ✓ Overcoming bad habits
- ✓ Overcoming limiting beliefs.

NLP is constantly evolving from the observations of behavior and communication of individuals. A variety of techniques and presuppositions are derived from these techniques of gathering data.

Further, these presuppositions are assumptions or central principles made by people and are useful in implementing change. These changes come in the form of them changing themselves or others.

Someone who is going through an NLP process has to believe these assumptions are true:

1. They already have all the resources they need. In other words, a person already has within them what they need—it is just a matter of putting it to use.
2. Every person does things with a positive intent. Look for the positive intentions in any behavior.
3. There is no such thing as a failure. People learn from mistakes. It is how someone deals with those mistakes. A person has to have the persistence to keep trying. Inherently, most people learn from their mistakes and don't make them again.
4. People are in charge of their own minds and in turn it means they are also in charge of their own actions and results. Take responsibility for your own actions and don't blame others.
5. Positive vs. Negative thinking: think positively as negative thinking can affect body functions and performance.

6. Respect: always respect another person's model of the world. An individual will carry around their own world experiences so a person needs to respect those. In conjunction with that, an individual has his own set of assumptions and beliefs and will create their own unique world around themselves.
7. Choice vs. no choice. Any option is better than having no options at all.
8. If something isn't working, do or try something else. Be flexible.
9. If something is possible, there has to be a way to do it. If someone can do it, someone can learn it.
10. Body Language plays an important role in a person's social and personal life. People use verbal and non-verbal body language to communicate so pay attention.

Chapter 2: Five NLP Techniques for a Fulfilling Life

There are five effective NLP techniques that can be used to change behavior, get better results and attract more positive experiences:

1. Belief Change. Negative experiences can cause someone to dwell on those experiences. If you believe that someone is prone to negative experiences, they will start to attract more, similar negative experiences only reaffirming themselves that they are prone to doom and gloom.

   At this point, it is better if someone were to get help to "reframe" these thoughts and not focus on the negative aspects all the time. A great way to rid someone of these negative beliefs is to spend a small amount of time each day with "affirmations."

   An affirmation will allow the person to come up with a completely different belief. Have them do this without any distractions—no phone, no TV, no cell phone, no family members—just quiet, alone time. Have them focus on their words and deeply take in their true meanings.

2. Anchoring. Anchoring is used to get an emotional response out of someone for something that they do or say. Have you ever seen someone unconsciously smile when they are touched for instance on their back or shoulder? To anchor someone, you have to first identify

the state you want them to experience and then do what it takes to get them into that state.

Touch them, again, on say their back or shoulder, and then remember the exact area you touched. Then, start talking to the person about some completely random subject to take their mind off of the previous activity.

Then, when the other person is completely off course from the touching exercise, touch them again in the same area and see what their response is to the touch. If you have performed this process successfully, the person should have the same emotional response as the one you wanted him/her to have.

3. Disassociation. If someone reacts to something in a negative way, it can cause them stress, negative emotions or depression. The emotion has to be gotten rid of in this case and the first thing to do is to identify the emotion.

    Go through the encounter with the person from start to finish so you can see what happens. Then have them play the movie backwards in their head. Then, fast-forward it and then play it backwards again repeating this several time. This is just like a recorder with a cassette tape inside it. Then, add a variable such as funny music. Then have the person picture the same event as if it were happening now.

They should have less of an initial response than they did before. The negative emotion should be gone and if not, have them repeat this process until the negative emotion has completely disappeared.

4. <u>Rapport</u>. Rapport means being able to get along with any type of person. This is fairly simple in that you can mirror someone's body language (but don't be too obvious), use similar words, have the same breathing pattern, etc.

   Anything that mirrors what the other person is doing so that you are "in sync" with the other person is building rapport. Another method of using rapport is by assessing what type of sensory perception the other person is using.

   The sensory perceptions are visual (your thoughts having to do with sight, spatial awareness and mental imagery), kinesthetic (feelings relating to the body such as pressure, temperature or emotion) or auditory/linguistic (relating to speech, white noise, dialog or sound).

5. <u>Content reframe</u>. This is used to stop what the person is doing and look at the situation in a totally new light when they feel hopeless, angry or some other negative emotion.

   Get the person to not focus on the negative parts of the situation but rather on the benefits. A great example of this would be if someone has just been fired from their job. Maybe they wanted to quit for a long time but didn't know how to or were too scared. Instead of being a victim, reframing the content of their thoughts will allow them to explore different opportunities that they might not otherwise have done.

Chapter 3: The Four Pillars of NLP

NLP has a framework of beliefs and attitudes which together form its model. These "presuppositions" can be considered as principles for living.

Outcomes: Since birth every person in the world has been asked the question, "What do you want?" And the answer always seems to be, "I don't know."

Where does this leave them? Drifting through life with no clear sense of direction or floating/drifting from one thing to the next leaves someone without a clear purpose. You have to know what you want before you can get it.

In the normal context of that question, you hear the words "aim," "goals," or "targets." Believe it or not, there are a lot of people wandering around who have none of the above. Within the confines of NLP the term is "outcome."

If a person knows their outcomes, they will have a better sense of the resources they will need to achieve that outcome. At any one time most people will have many different outcomes relating to various aspects of their life.

And, in defining outcomes, if they are well-formed, someone will have all the details and can imagine what it's like to have already attained that outcome. In other words, the more clearly they know what they want, the more likely they are to get it.

Rapport: This is the secret ingredient in establishing and maintaining relationships. People who have said, "I feel on the same wavelength," or "it just feels right to us," or they have "hit it off" with someone are all expressions used in describing rapport.

Rapport is a skill that can be enhanced and developed over time by doing things such as adapting our communication to suit the other person or altering our body language to match theirs.

Having the skill to be able to sit and listen without interrupting someone and then respecting their view can be considered rapport.

There is also the rapport we have with ourselves, in particular the rapport between our conscious and unconscious minds. This is that feeling of being torn with part of us wanting to do one thing and another part wanting to do another.

Inner peace comes with having greater rapport with the various aspects of yourself.

Behavioral Flexibility: If the actions you are taking are not leading you in the direction you want to go it's obvious that you should try something different.

If you keep on doing the same thing you are thought to have a lack of behavioral flexibility meaning that you are going to keep on doing the same thing which in turn will cause you to get the same results. What most people don't realize or understand is that by conscious choice, at any given moment, they can turn anything around.

A lot of people feel it is safer to stay where they are rather than try something new even if they continually get the wrong results.

Sensory Awareness or Acuity: This is defined as someone who is able to be alert to fine details and keen observation and be extremely aware of what is going on around them. This gives you information about whether what you are doing is giving you what you want, i.e. moving you closer to your outcomes or not.

This pillar makes you use your senses in order to be aware of what is going on around you. How much do people really notice by looking, listening and feeling?

Some people are extremely observant while others seem to have their head in the clouds all the time (or their cell phone these days). If someone was told to close their eyes right at this second, how much of what is around them do you think they could describe? If they are like most people, they probably couldn't describe much at all.

This sensory acuity pillar is important in that it gives you information so you will know that what you are doing is giving you what you want (your outcomes).

It is also important for use in the business world or dealing with others. You are aware of their expressions, body language and voice tone.

A number of NLP "change techniques" involve discovering the positive intention of a behavior and finding alternative ways of satisfying it. There is always a purpose, a reason, "positive intention" behind every Behavior which arises when the behavior is first established. (i.e. smoking at 14 in order to feel grown up).

Any behavior, no matter how strange it may seem, was the best choice available to the person at that moment in time, given their life history, knowledge, beliefs and resources, and viewed from their frame of reference.

Knowing the outcome you want in any situation greatly increases your ability to achieve it. Eliminating what doesn't work can be an effective way of finding out what does. The more failures you have, the more you learn.

Outcomes can be small and short-term or large and long-term………………………

TO FIND OUT MORE ABOUT NLP VISIT

WWW.RETIREEARLYPRODUCTIONS.COM

www.ingramcontent.com/pod-product-compliance
Lightning Source LLC
Chambersburg PA
CBHW070357190526
45169CB00003B/1035